Commissioned by Worthing Choral Society, conductor Aedan Kerr and first performed on 15 November 2014 at St George's Church, St George's Road, Worthing, West Sussex

T0071042

A Winter's Night

Christmas Cantata

for SATB, brass quintet, percussion and organ

1. In Dulci Jubilo

CECILIA McDOWALL

German, 14th cent.
Translation: R.L. Pearsall

With exuberance, dancing ♩. = 63

ORGAN

f *mf* Ped.

6 *f* *mp* Man. Ped. *mf*

11 *mp* Man.

15 *mf* Ped.

© Oxford University Press 2014
OXFORD UNIVERSITY PRESS, MUSIC DEPARTMENT, GREAT CLARENDON STREET, OXFORD OX2 6DP.
Photocopying this copyright material is ILLEGAL

20
cresc. poco a poco
2
1
25
S.
A.
unis. f
1. In dul - ci ju - bi - lo, -bi - lo, -bi - lo,
T.
B.
unis. f
1. In dul - ci ju - bi - lo, -bi-lo, -bi-lo,
f
Man.
31
Now sing with hearts a - glow, with hearts a - glow.
Nun sing - et und seid froh, seid froh, seid froh.
-bi-lo,
Now sing with hearts a - glow, with hearts a - glow, a-glow.
Nun sing - et und seid froh, seid froh, seid froh, seid froh.

CHRISTMAS CHORAL WORKS

SATB (with divisions), brass quintet, percussion, and organ

OXFORD

A Winter's Night

Christmas Cantata

Cecilia McDowall

MUSIC DEPARTMENT

OXFORD
UNIVERSITY PRESS

37
mf
Our de-light and plea-sure Lies in prae-se-pi-o Like sun-shine is our trea-sure Ma-
Un-sers Her-zens Won-ne Leit Und leuch-tet als die Son-ne
mf
Our de-light and plea-sure Lies in prae-se-pi-o Like sun-shine is our trea-sure Ma-
Un-sers Her-zens Won-ne Leit Und leuch-tet als die Son-ne
mf
43
mp cresc.
O,
f
-tris in gre-mi-o, Al-pha es et O, Al-pha es et O!
mp cresc.
f
-tris in gre-mi-o, Al-pha es et O, Al-pha es et O!
mp cresc.
f
Ped.

49
2
unis.
mp
2. O Je - su par - vu - le, -vu-
unis.
mp
2. O Je - su par - vu - le, -vu- le,
mp
Man.
55
- le, -vu - le,
For thee I long al - way, al - way, al-
Nach dir ist mir so weh, so weh, so
-vu-le, -vu-le,
For thee I long al - way, al - way, al - way,
Nach dir ist mir so weh, so weh, so weh,

61
mf
- way, Com-fort my heart's blind-ness, O Pu - er op - ti - me, With all thy lov - ing
weh. Tröst mir mein Ge - mü - te, Durch al - le dei - ne
mf
al-way: Com-fort my heart's blind-ness, O Pu - er op - ti - me, With all thy lov - ing
so weh. Tröst mir mein Ge - mü - te, Durch al - le dei - ne
mf

67
mp cresc.
te.
- kind - nĕss, O Prin-ceps glo-ri - ae! Tra - he me post te, post te, Tra - he me post
Gü - te,
mp cresc.
post te,
- kind - ness, O Prin-ceps glo-ri - ae! Tra - he me post te, Tra - he me post
Gü - te,
mp cresc.

73
mf
te.
mf
te.
mf
(Man.)
78
3
S.
p dolce
p
3. O Pa - tris ca - ri - tas, -ri-tas, O Na - ti le - ni-
A.
p dolce
p
3. O Pa - tris ca - ri - tas, o Pa - tris ca - ri - tas, O Na - ti le - ni-
p dolce
p

84
mf
- tas, -ni-tas!
Deep-ly were we stain - èd
Wir wärn all' ver - lo - ren
Per nos - tra cri-mi -
- tas, o Na - ti le - ni - tas!
Deep-ly were we stain - èd
Wir wärn all' ver - lo - ren
Per nos - tra cri-mi -
Deep-ly were we stain - èd
Wir wärn all' ver - lo - ren
Per nos - tra cri-mi -

90
mp cresc.
- na;
But thou for us hast gain - èd
So hat er uns er - wor - ben
Coe - lo - rum gau-di - a.
O that we were
Ei - a, wärn wir
- na;
But thou for us hast gain - èd
So hat er uns er - wor - ben
Coe - lo - rum gau-di - a.
O that we were
Ei - a, wärn wir
mp cresc.

96
O.
there, O, O that we were there.
da, ei - a, ei - a, wärn wir da!
there, O, O that we were there.
da, ei - a, ei - a, wärn wir da!
Ped.
101
4
S.
4. U - bi sunt gau - di - a, gau- gau-di-, gau - di - a,
In
A.
4. U - bi sunt gau - di - a, gau - di - a, -di - a,
In
unis.
T.
B.
4. U - bi sunt gau - di - a, -di-a, -di-a, -di-a,
In

107
an - y place but there, but there, but there? There are an - gels
Nir-gends mehr denn da, denn da, denn da? Da die En - gel
an - y place but there, but there in an - y place but there? There are an - gels
Nir-gends mehr denn da, denn da, nir - gends mehr denn da? Da die En - gel
an - y place but there, but there, but there, but there? There are an - gels
Nir-gends mehr denn da, denn da, da, denn da? Da die En - gel
an - y place but there, but there, but there? There are an - gels
Nir-gends mehr denn da, denn da, da? Da die En - gel
(Ped.)
113
sing - ing No - va can - ti - ca, And there the bells are ring - ing, In
sing - en Und die Schel - len kling - en
sing - ing No - va can - ti - ca, And there the bells are ring - ing, In
sing - en Und die Schel - len kling - en
sing - ing No - va can - ti - ca, And there the bells are ring - ing, In
sing - en Und die Schel - len kling - en
sing - ing No - va can - ti - ca, And there the bells are ring - ing, In
sing - en Und die Schel - len kling - en

118
Re - gis cu - ri - a.
O that we were there.
Ei - a, wärn wir da,
Re - gis cu - ri - a.
O that we were there, o, o that we were there.
Ei - a, wärn wir da, ei - a, ei - a, wärn wir da.
Re - gis cu - ri - a.
O that we were there, o, o that we were there.
Ei - a, wärn wir da, ei - a, ei - a, wärn wir da.
Re - gis cu - ri - a.
O that we were there, o that we were there.
Ei - a, wärn wir da, ei - a, wärn wir da.
124
poco a poco rit.
poco a poco rit.
mf
Man.

2. O little one sweet

Translation: Percy Dearmer

17th-century German melody

153
sweet, O lit - tle one mild.
süss, O Je - su - lein mild.
mp cantabile
Ped.
6
159
S.
p legatissimo
2. O lit - tle one sweet, O lit - tle one mild, With joy thou
2. O Je - su-lein süss, O Je - su-lein mild, Mit Freu - den
A.
p legatissimo (stagger breathing, if necessary)
2. ah ah ah
T.
p legatissimo (stagger breathing, if necessary)
2. ah ah ah
B.
p legatissimo (stagger breathing, if necessary)
2. ah ah
[optional accompaniment]
p legatissimo

165
hast the whole world filled; Thou cam - est here from heav'n's do -
hast du die Welt er - füllt. Du kommst he - rab vom Him - mels -
ah
ah
ah
171
- main, To bring men com - fort in their pain, O lit - tle one
- saal, Und tröst'st uns in dem Jam - mer - thal, O Je - su - lein
ah
ah
ah
ah
ah
ah

177
sweet, O lit - tle one mild.
süss, O Je - su-lein mild.
mp cantabile
Ped.
7
183
p espress.
3. ah ah
p espress.
3. ah ah
p
3. O lit - tle one sweet, O lit - tle one mild, In thee love's
3. O Je - su-lein süss, O Je - su-lein mild, Du bist der
p
3. O lit - tle one sweet, O lit - tle one mild, In thee love's
3. O Je - su-lein süss, O Je - su-lein mild, Du bist der
p
Man.

189
ah
ah
ah
beau - ties are all dis - tilled; Then light in us thy love's bright
Lieb ein We - ben - bild; Zünd an in uns der Lie - be
beau - ties are all dis - tilled; Then light in us thy love's bright
Lieb ein We - ben - bild; Zünd an in uns der Lie - be
195
ah
lit - tle one
Je - su - lein
ah
ah
lit - tle one
Je - su - lein
flame, That we may give thee back the same, O lit - tle one
Flamm, Dass wir dich lieb - en all - zu - samm, O Je - su - lein
flame, That we may give thee back the same, O lit - tle one
Flamm, Dass wir dich lieb - en all - zu - samm, O Je - su - lein

201
sweet, O lit - tle one mild.
süss, O Je - su-lein mild.
sweet, O lit - tle one mild.
süss, O Je - su - lein mild.
sweet, O lit - tle one mild.
süss, O Je - su - lein mild.
sweet, O lit - tle one mild.
süss, O Je - su - lein mild.
mp cresc.
Ped.
3. Noël Nouvelet
French Traditional, 15th cent.
207
ad lib.
8
Bright, rhythmic ♩ = 92 (♪ = ♪ sempre)
f marcato ma leggiero
Man.
211

SOPRANOS & ALTOS
214
mf
1. No - ël nou-ve - let! No - ël chan-tons i - ci Dé - vo - tes gens, ren-
mf
220
- dons à Dieu mer - ci; Chan-tons No - ël pour le Roi nou - ve - let:
226
9
No - ël nou-ve - let! No - ël chan-tons i - ci.
f
Man.
TENORS & BASSES
f
232
Qui aux pas - teurs di-
2. D'un oi - sil - lon a - près le chant j'ou - ï Qui aux pas - teurs di-

238
- sait: 'Par-tez d'i - ci; En Beth-lé - em trou - ve-rez l'an-ge - let.' No -
244
10
- ël nou-ve - let! No - ël chan-tons i - ci.
250
DESCANT (SOPRANOS)
mf
S.
3. No-ël nou-ve - let! No - ël chan-tons i - ci, No - ël, no-
ALL OTHER VOICES
mf
ALL VOICES
3. En_ Beth-lé - em, Ma - rie et_ Jo-seph vy L'âne et le
mf
Ped.

256
-ël, l'En - fant cou - ché par - mi; La crêche é - tait au lieu d'un ber - ce -
boeuf, l'En - fant cou - ché par - mi; La crêche é - tait au lieu d'un ber - ce -
262
11
- let, No - ël nou-ve - let! No - ël chan - tons i - ci.
- let, No-ël nou-ve - let! No - ël chan-tons i - ci.
f
Man.
Ped.
268
SOPRANOS & ALTOS
f
4. Bien - tôt les rois, par l'é - toile é-clair-

274
S.
A.
- cis
TENORS & BASSES
T.
B.
4. De l'o - ri - ent dont ils é - taient sor - tis A Beth-lé -
280
No - ël, no - ël nou - ve - let! No - ël chan-tons i -
- em vin - rent un ma - ti - net. No - ël nou - ve - let! No - ël chan-tons i -
12
286
unis.
-ci.
5. L'un por - tait l'or, et
-ci.
Man.
Ped.

291
l'au - tre myrrh aus - si,
Et l'au-tr'en - cens, que fais - ait bon sen -
296
-ti: No - ël, no - ël, no - ël, no - ël, no-
-ti: Le pa-ra - dis sem - blait le jar-di - net. No-ël nou-ve - let! No-
-ti: Le pa-ra - dis sem - blait le jar-di - net. No-ël nou-ve - let! No-
-ti: Le pa-ra - dis sem - blait le jar-di - net. No-ël nou-ve - let! No-
Man.
Ped.

303
-ël, no - ël, No - ël, no - ël, no -
-ël chan-tons i - ci, No - ël nou-ve - let! No - ël chan-tons i -
-ël chan-tons i - ci, No - ël nou-ve - let! No - ël chan-tons i -
-ël chan - tons i - ci, No - ël nou-ve - let! No - ël chan - tons i -
308
poco a poco rit.
- ël!
- ci.
- ci.
- ci.
poco a poco rit.
mf
Man.

4. Still, still, still

Austrian carol (1819)
Translation: Angier Brock

14
329
S.
will!
still.
p
2. Schlaf,
2. ah
A.
p
2. Schlaf, mein
2. Sleep, sleep
T.
p
2. Schlaf, schlaf, schlaf, mein
2. Sleep, sleep, sleep, sleep
B.
p
2. Schlaf, schlaf, schlaf, mein
2. Sleep, sleep, sleep, sleep
mp cantabile
p
Ped.
335
schlaf, schlaf, schlaf,
ah ah ah
lie - bes Kind - lein, schlaf! Die Eng' - lein tun schön mu - si - zie - ren, vor dem Kind-lein
well in Ma - ry's arms. The star of the Ma - gi shines high a-bove you. An - gels are sing-ing,
Kind - lein, schlaf! Die Eng' - lein tun schön mu - si - zie - ren, vor dem Kind-lein
well in Ma - ry's arms. The star of the Ma - gi shines high a-bove you. An - gels are sing-ing,
lie - bes Kind-lein, schlaf! ah
well in Ma - ry's arms. ah

340
Schlaf, schlaf!
ah ah
ju - bi - lie - ren. Schlaf, mein lie - bes Kind - lein, schlaf!
oh, how they love you! Sleep, sleep well in Ma - ry's arms.
ju - bi - lie - ren. Schlaf, schlaf, schlaf, mein Kind - lein, schlaf!
oh, how they love you! Sleep, sleep, sleep, sleep well in Ma - ry's arms.
Schlaf, schlaf, schlaf, mein lie - bes Kind-lein, schlaf!
Sleep, sleep, sleep, sleep well in Ma - ry's arms.
15
345
p
3. Gross, gross, gross, die Lieb ist
3. Joy, joy, joy, take joy, take
p
3. Gross, gross, gross, die Lieb ist üb - er -
3. Joy, joy, joy, take joy in the green-ing of
p
3. Gross, gross,
3. Joy, joy,
p
3. mm
mp cantabile
p
Man.
Ped.

351
üb - er-gross, gross, gross.
joy, joy, joy.
-gross. Gott hat den Him-mels-thron ver - las - sen und muss rei - sen auf der Strass-en.
love. God comes to live our hu - man sto - ry, comes as a child, re - lin-quish-ing glo - ry.
gross. Gott hat den Him-mels-thron ver - las - sen und muss rei - sen auf der Strass-en.
love. God comes to live our hu - man sto - ry, comes as a child, re - lin-quish-ing glo - ry.
mm
356
Gross, gross, gross, die Lieb ist üb - er - gross.
Joy, joy, joy, take joy in love.
Gross, gross, gross, die Lieb ist üb - er - gross.
Joy, joy, joy, take joy in the green-ing of love.
Gross, gross.
Joy, joy.
mm
mm
mp
Man.

16
361
SOPRANOS (& optional ALTOS)
unis.
p
4. Wir, wir, wir, wir ru - fen all zu
4. Dream, dream, dream, dream now in the full-ness of
pp
366
dir: Tu uns des Him - mels Reich auf-schlies-sen, wenn wir ein - mal ster - ben müs - sen.
time. No need to - night for wor - ry or warn - ing. Win - ter's sun will rise in the morn - ing.
371
pp
Wir, wir, wir, wir ru - fen all zu dir, wir ru - fen all zu
Dream, dream, dream, dream now in the full-ness of time, dream now in the full-ness of

376
S.
dir.
time.
Schlaf, schlaf!
ah ah
A.
Schlaf, mein lie - bes Kind - lein, schlaf!
Sleep, sleep well in Ma - ry's arms.
T.
Schlaf, schlaf, schlaf, mein Kind - lein, schlaf!
Sleep, sleep, sleep, sleep well in Ma - ry's arms.
B.
Schlaf, schlaf, schlaf, mein lie - bes Kind-lein, schlaf!
Sleep, sleep, sleep, sleep well in Ma - ry's arms.
Ped.
poco rit.
Energetic, with joy ♩. = 76
381
Man.
385
Ped.

5. Sussex Carol

Traditional English, 17th cent.

404
♪ = ♪ sempre
hear the news the an - gels bring, On Christ-mas night all Christ-ians sing, To hear the news the
Solo
409
mf
f
an - gels bring. News of great joy, news of great mirth, News of our
end solo
mf
f
Ped.
414
mf
18
S.
A.
mer-ci- ful King's birth.
T.
B.
mf
f
2. Then
mp
Man.
Ped.

419
mf
mm
mm
why should men on earth be so sad, Since our Re - deem - er made us glad, Then why should men on
424
mf
When from our sin he set us
mf
earth be so sad, Since our Re - deem - er made us glad, When from our sin he set us
mf
429
ah
f
free, All for to gain our li - ber - ty.
f
free, All for to gain our li - ber - ty.
f

19
434
SOPRANOS & ALTOS
unis.
mp dolce
S.
A.
3.When sin de-parts be - fore his grace, Then life and health come
mp legato
Man.
439
in its place, When sin de - parts be - fore his grace, Then life and health come
443
p
mf ah
in its place; An - gels and men with joy may sing, All for to
TENORS & BASSES
T.
B.
An - gels and men with joy may sing, All for to
Ped.

20
448
see the new - born King.
see the new - born King.
mp
Man.
452
DESCANT (SOPRANOS)
S.
f
4. All out of dark - ness we have light, Which
ALL VOICES
ALL OICES
f
4. All out of dark - ness we have light, Which
f
Ped.
456
made an-gels sing, All out of dark - ness we have light, Which
made the an - gels sing this night, All out of dark - ness we have light, Which

460
SOPRANOS & ALTOS
made an - gels sing:
Glo - ry to God and
TENORS & BASSES
made the an - gels sing this night:
Glo - ry to God and peace to
464
peace, and peace to men, and glo - ry to God and
unis.
men, Glo - ry to God and peace to
468
there,
peace, and peace to men, O that we were there, O,
men, peace to men, O that we were there,

472
O that we were there.
Glo - ry to
O that we were there.
477
God and peace to men,
Now and for ev - er -
allargando
allargando
482
a tempo
ff
more. A - men.
ff
a tempo
ff

OXFORD CAROLS

Oxford publishes a vast array of Christmas music to suit every occasion and choir. There are pieces and collections for services, concerts, and carol-singing; pieces for SATB, upper-voice, and unison choirs; *a cappella* carols and carols with piano or organ accompaniment; and a wealth of traditional favourites alongside new carols by leading composers. There are also over 250 orchestrations of carols from *Carols for Choirs* and other collections available for hire, including versions for brass, strings, and full orchestra. With hundreds of individual titles and an impressive range of carol anthologies, Oxford provides a rich collection of the very best in Christmas music.

Selected carol anthologies from Oxford University Press

Carols for Choirs 1–5

The Oxford Book of Flexible Carols
Edited by Alan Bullard

For Him all Stars, 15 carols for upper voices

A Merry Little Christmas, 12 popular classics for choirs
Compiled and edited by Jerry Rubino

An American Christmas, 16 carols and carol arrangements from North America
Compiled and edited by Jerry Rubino

An Edwardian Carol Book, 12 carols for mixed voices
Selected and edited by Jeremy Dibble

Alan Bullard Carols, 10 carols for mixed voices

Bob Chilcott Carols 1, 9 carols for mixed voices

Bob Chilcott Carols 2, 10 carol arrangements for mixed voices

John Gardner Carols, 11 carols for mixed voices

John Rutter Carols, 10 carols for mixed voices

Mack Wilberg Carols, 8 carol arrangements for mixed voices

World Carols for Choirs, SATB and upper-voice editions
Compiled and edited by Bob Chilcott and Susan Knight

Christmas Spirituals for Choirs
Compiled and edited by Bob Chilcott and Ken Burton

The Ivy and the Holly, 14 contemporary carols

OXFORD
UNIVERSITY PRESS

www.oup.com

ISBN 978-0-19-340368-0

9 780193 403680